Westminster Abbey 900 Years

THE DEAN AND CHAPTER

Dean
The Very Rev. Eric S. Abbott, M.A., D.D. (1959)
Archdeacon, Treasurer and Lector Theologiae
The Ven. E. F. Carpenter, M.A., B.D., PH.D. (1951)
Steward and Chronicler
The Rev. Canon M. S. Stancliffe, M.A. (1957)
Sub-Dean
The Rev. Canon M. A. C. Warren, M.A., D.D. (1963)
The Rt. Rev. Joost de Blank, M.A., D.D. (1964)
Chapter Clerk
W. R. J. Pullen, LL.B., F.C.I.S.

MINOR CANONS

Precentor
The Rev. R. Simpson (1963)
Sacrist
The Rev. C. Hildyard, M.A. (1932)
The Rev. G. R. Dunstan, M.A., F.S.A. (1959)

LAY OFFICERS

High Steward
The Rt. Hon. The Lord Clitheroe, P.C., M.A., F.S.A.
Deputy High Steward
The Rt. Worshipful The Mayor of Westminster
High Bailiff and Searcher of the Sanctuary
The Right Hon. Sir Henry Willink, Bt., M.C., Q.C., M.A., D.C.L., LL.D.
Deputy High Bailiff
G. G. Hartwright
Receiver-General, Chapter Clerk and Registrar
W. R. J. Pullen, LL.B., F.C.I.S.
Legal Secretary
J. S. Widdows, M.B.E.
Organist and Master of the Choristers
Douglas Guest, M.A., MUS.B., F.R.C.M., Hon.R.A.M., A.R.C.O.
Auditor
Sir William Lawson, C.B.E., F.C.A.
Surveyor of the Fabric
S. E. Dykes Bower, M.A., F.R.I.B.A., F.S.A.
Librarian and Keeper of the Muniments
L. E. Tanner, C.V.O., M.A., F.S.A.
Headmaster of the Choir School
F. J. Tullo, M.A.

WESTMINSTER SCHOOL

Head Master
J. D. Carleton, M.A.
Under Master and Master of the Queen's Scholars
J. S. Woodhouse, M.A.

Text. The Dean and Chapter of Westminster.

Design and Production. Roger and Robert Nicholson, London.

Printed in Great Britain by Westerham Press.

Correct at time of going to press September 21, 1965.

Message from Her Majesty The Queen

Visitor of Westminster Abbey

On the occasion of the 900th anniversary of the Dedication of Westminster Abbey, I join with the Dean and Chapter of Westminster in the thanksgiving which they are offering to Almighty God for the witness to God's Sovereignty and the Gospel of Christ which the Abbey has borne throughout the centuries, both in monastic times and since the Reformation. In particular, I am bound to recall my own Coronation in the great Church which has seen the crowning of so many Kings and Queens since the Coronation of William the Conqueror on Christmas Day, 1066.

I send to the Dean and Chapter my heartfelt good wishes for their work at the present time, and pray that through the years to come Westminster Abbey may serve the cause of Christian unity, inspire our national life, and be a focal point for the spiritual life and aspirations of a great multitude of people.

The Theme for 1966 'One People'

The Ven. E. F. Carpenter, M.A., B.D., Ph.D.
Archdeacon of Westminster

Westminster Abbey has a very long history and has consequently entered into a rich and many sided inheritance. This history stretches back to that day on 28 December 1065, when the church, built by Edward the Confessor, then on his deathbed, was consecrated and dedicated to St. Peter, and a Benedictine Community was established within its walls. Indeed even before that time, though its precise history is shrouded in mystery, some kind of a religious house existed on this site upon the marshes of Thorney Island.

This history of nine hundred years has had great and formative moments making for challenge and fresh opportunity. The original Norman church was pulled down by Henry III in the middle of the thirteenth century and a more magnificent Gothic building, which still excites awe and wonder, gradually arose in its stead. At the time of the Reformation, the Benedictine monastery with some five hundred years of history behind it was dissolved, and Queen Elizabeth refounded it as the Collegiate Church of St. Peter in Westminster. Such it has remained to this day.

Yet a noble inheritance is not preserved by a nostalgic reflection upon past glories. Faithfulness and loyalty demand something more. It is as true of institutions as it is of persons that they either progress or regress; they go forward or they retreat; they stretch out from the present to greet and help fashion the future, or they withdraw and petrify.

The history of Westminster Abbey has been one of involvement. The Benedictines seeking order and stability yet engaged in their worship close to the seats of power and government. Coronations and the burial of kings gave to their church a particular character, and linked it up with the life of a nation, a link that has grown more intimate and at the same time wider in its scope as the centuries have gone on. Whatever we may think of the many memorials as works of art they yet remind us that the fitful life of man, even in its greatest achievements, needs to be commended to the mercy of God; and that the kingdoms of this world need to be measured against the 'city which hath foundations'.

Therefore as Westminster Abbey celebrates with thanksgiving nine hundred years of continuing existence and brings into focus some of the great moments of its history, it is imperative that it looks from within outwards in order to be true to an ancient inheritance. Its concern must be with man in the present, submitted as he is to the stresses and changes of a challenging world; and also with what the Spirit of the living God is saying to this generation. For this reason the Abbey has taken a theme for the year which arises out of its own past. The theme is '*One People*'.

Now that modern technology has annihilated distance and men of different colours, creeds and ideologies confront each other as never before, it is dangerously easy to see this new situation only as the occasion of strife and

Kenya Independence Day Service at Westminster Abbey.

Opposite: The Wilton Diptych, (detail, by courtesy of the National Gallery). This portrays Edward the Confessor as a saint, to the left of St. John the Baptist, with Richard II kneeling in front of them.

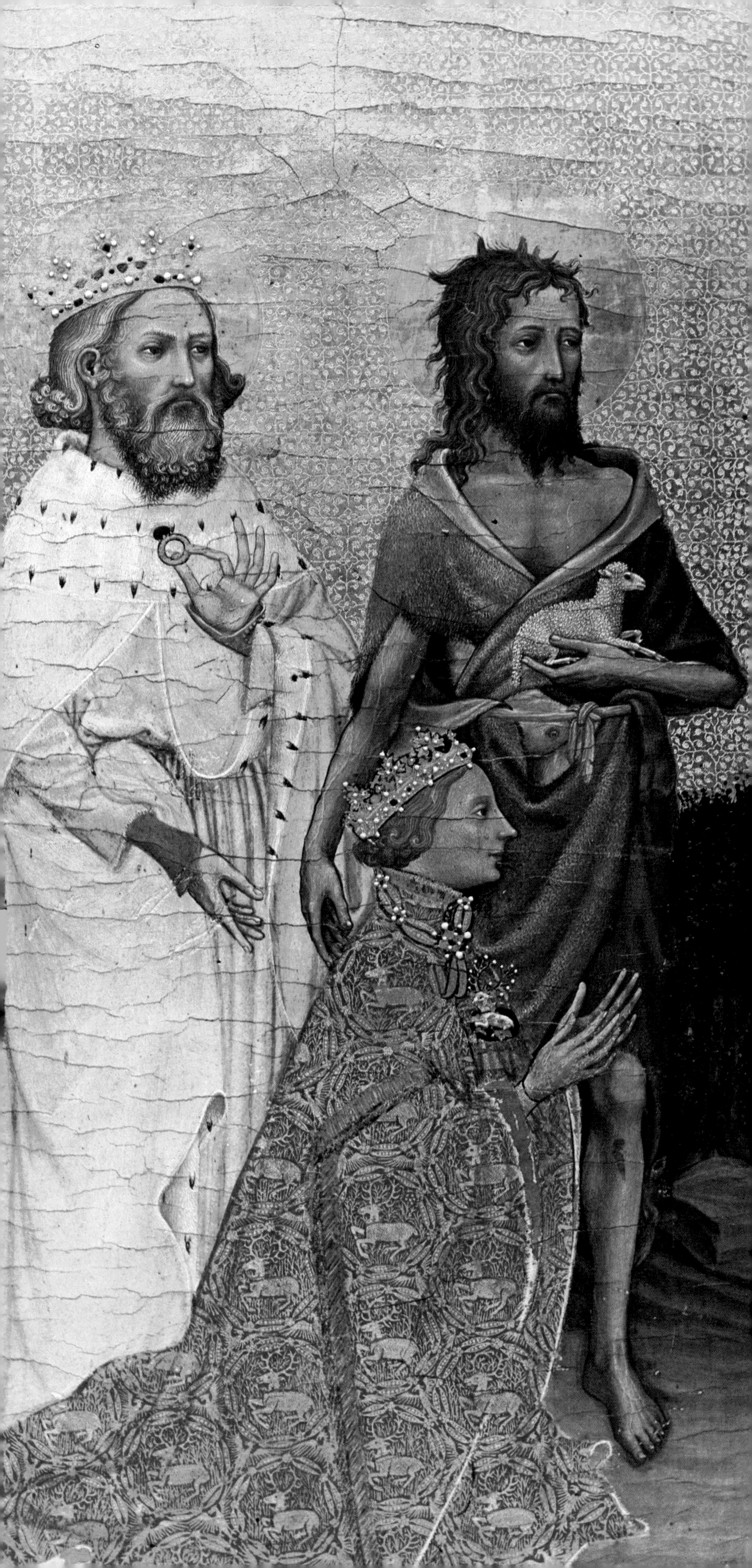

Queen Elizabeth I
(by courtesy of the National Portrait Gallery).

Queen Mary I
(by courtesy of the National Portrait Gallery).

division. Yet within this same world, painfully in travail, a new order is struggling to be born.

Those who belong to 'the congregation of Christian people dispersed throughout the world' are becoming aware of each other as belonging to one family – the great new fact of our time, as the late Archbishop Temple described it. The older religions of the East are offering, from within their own treasure house of spirituality, new riches for the West. The United Nations, with its agencies for relief and rehabilitation, is slowly, despite bitter frustration and disappointment, building up patterns of justice between nations and respect for law. God's spirit is equally at work within the intellectual ferment of our day, and in our modern science and technology. Indeed, we make a great mistake if we think in terms of two separate cultures.

The concern of Westminster Abbey, in this year, when it thankfully remembers its own history of involvement, is therefore to come behind, to help to quicken, and to commend all the activities of men directed towards making one people, activities which the Spirit is calling forth. Through acts of worship and the regular rhythm of prayer which have been, across the centuries, its primary activity; through exhibitions in the Chapter House during the whole of 1966, the Abbey will seek to encourage the hope of a world made one, while at the same time it fosters a dedication which will help to build it. To be made aware of the work of committed men in richly diverse areas of human endeavour may help to renew that vision, without which people and nations perish.

History, alas, is not always a cordial for drooping spirits: and there is certainly much around us which could lead to the pessimism that invites disaster – the clash of race and colour, competing ideologies, affluence existing alongside poverty, iron curtains and apartheid. Dr. Gilbert Murray, who is buried in the Abbey, says of Greek society that it finally succumbed to a 'failure of nerve'. It is, however, from within the conviction that God is working his purpose out as year succeeds to year, that the Abbey has realistically and soberly selected as its theme for 1966 '*One People*'.

Thomas Babington Macaulay, also buried in the Abbey, described it as that 'temple of silence and reconciliation where the enmities of a thousand years lie buried'. Those of us who are privileged to serve Westminster Abbey in 1966 would like to think that this period of celebration will help to bring reconciliation in life rather than in the stillness of the tomb; and that the year will not only see the thankful remembrance of a past history, but a present generation stirred to hope and challenged to high endeavour.

Preceding page: The Rose Window in the South Transept.

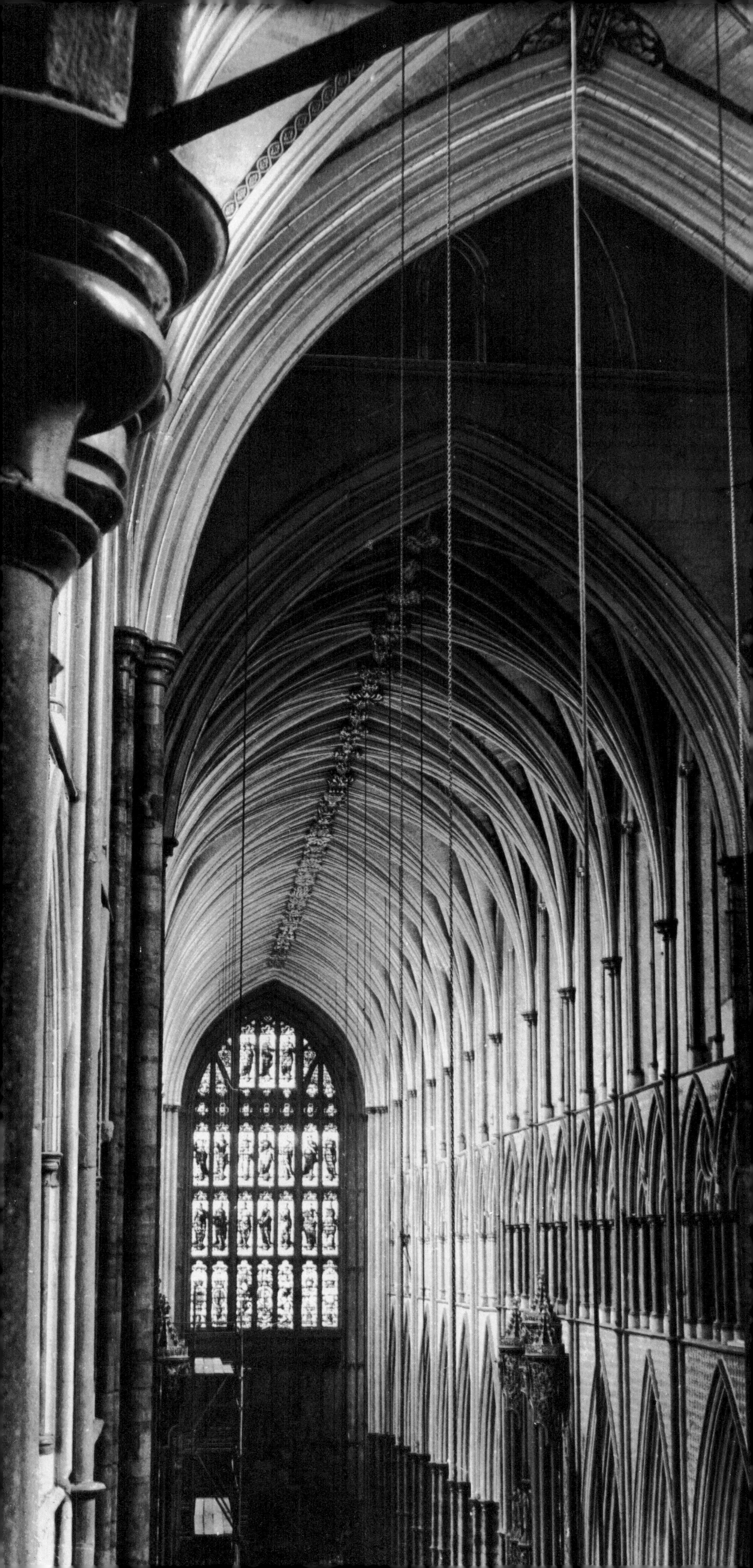

White
Till Yard
Pallace Yard
Westmr St
Old Pallace Yard
Deanes yarde

The History

L. E. Tanner, C.V.O., M.A., F.S.A.
Librarian and Keeper of the Muniments

In the most remote times there was an island in the Thames called Thorney or the Isle of Thorns. It was some thirty acres in extent; a desolate spot with nothing to suggest that one day it would become famous throughout the world as the very centre of what we now call Westminster.

Tradition and legend have become so entangled that it is impossible to say when a Christian Church was built upon the island, but we are on fairly safe ground if we say that by the 10th century there had been a church with a small monastery attached to it established there for a considerable time.

No trace has ever been found of this first Abbey Church, but it is believed to have stood just west of the present Church. Its importance lies in the fact that by 1042 when Edward the Confessor ascended the throne Thorney was already considered to be a specially sacred spot, and it was this fact that led the Confessor to reconstruct the primitive church on a far grander scale. To watch the progress of the building became the great interest of his declining years, and he lived just long enough to see his new church consecrated on Holy Innocents Day 1065. A few days later he was buried within its walls. Nothing now remains above ground of this great church, but it was far larger than any 11th century Norman church which has survived, and we know from foundations which still exist that its ground plan had an internal length of 322 ft. which is not much shorter than the present Abbey Church.

Edward the Confessor is rightly looked upon as the real founder of Westminster. It was due to the sanctity of his character and to the veneration in which the Confessor was held that William the Conqueror determined to be crowned in the new church, thereby setting a precedent which has ever since been followed, and that Westminster became the burial place of Kings. Moreover the proximity of the Palace, which was the principal residence of our medieval sovereigns, led to Westminster becoming a peculiarly royal church, and to the monastery which was attached to it becoming one of the greatest of the English Benedictine Monasteries.

Except for the addition of a Lady Chapel in 1220 the Confessor's Church stood untouched for nearly two hundred years. Then in 1245 Henry III, influenced not merely by his devotion to the Confessor's memory but by the beauty of the newly built French cathedrals such as Amiens and Rheims, determined to pull it down and build a new church more in accordance with the ideas of the time and as a setting for a splendid new Shrine for the Confessor. The East end, the Transepts and the Choir of the present Abbey Church were built, therefore, between 1245 and 1269, but the Nave of the Confessor's Church was left untouched until such time as money was forthcoming for it to be rebuilt. A hundred years later in 1375 that great work was undertaken under the supervision of the most celebrated of medieval 'architects', Henry Yevele. As it has been well

The effigy of King Henry III in Westminster Abbey.
Opposite : An engraving by William Southorne, based on a map by Richard Newcourt, 1658.

said 'he was original enough not to seek after originality', for he continued the building in the style of the earlier work, so that the Abbey gives the impression of being all of one date. Actually the work on the Nave was not finally completed until the early years of the 16th century.

Meanwhile, in 1503, the foundation stone of a new Lady Chapel was laid, and Henry VII's Chapel as it has come to be called, with its marvellously carved roof, has been called 'one of the most perfect buildings ever erected in England'. With its completion a few years later this long story of building and re-building at Westminster came to an end.

And then the blow fell. In 1540 the Monastery was dissolved, and with its dissolution there came to an end, save for a brief revival under Queen Mary I, at least six hundred years of monasticism at Westminster. At the same time the plate, vestments, stained glass and other treasures were ruthlessly swept away or destroyed. But the royal association with Westminster ensured that the Abbey Church itself remained intact, and when in 1561, the monastery was finally replaced by the Collegiate Church of St. Peter, Westminster, the new foundation retained many of its ancient privileges. Thenceforth it became the task of the Dean and Chapter to conserve the great church committed to their charge. Unfortunately still further damage was done during the Civil War and under the Commonwealth, and by the end of the 17th century Sir Christopher Wren had to undertake extensive repairs to the outside stonework. But the only major additions to the fabric were the western towers which were built by Hawksmoor and James between 1732 and 1745.

It has been said above that one of the objects which led Henry III to rebuild the Abbey Church was to provide a worthy setting for a new Shrine for Edward the Confessor. That great Shrine, with its Purbeck-marble base decorated with Italian Cosmati work and surmounted by a gold feretory containing the body of the Saint was completed in 1269. Although it was razed to the ground at the Dissolution and the gold feretory destroyed, the body of St. Edward was allowed to be reburied in an obscure grave and the stone composing the Shrine was also preserved. It was possible, therefore, during the brief restoration of the Monastery under Queen Mary I, for Abbot Feckenham to re-construct it as well as he could and to replace the body of the Saint within it, and the Shrine as we see it today was his work.

It has always been regarded as the most venerated spot within the Church. Around it are the splendid medieval tombs of Henry III, Edward I, Edward III, Philippa of Hainault, Richard II and Anne of Bohemia, and the Chantry Chapel and tomb of Henry V. The circle of tombs around the Shrine was complete by the end of the 15th century and in consequence it was Henry VII's intention to erect a tomb in his new Chapel to Henry VI. But it was not to be, and eventually the Chapel became Henry VII's own mausoleum with his great tomb, by the Italian Torrigiano, as its central feature. In the side aisles of this Chapel are the fine tombs of Elizabeth I and of Mary, Queen of Scots. It is, however, a remarkable fact that none of the later sovereigns buried in the Chapel (James I, Anne of Denmark, Charles

This page: The effigy of Edward III.
Opposite: The shrine of Edward the Confessor.

II, William III and Mary II, Anne, and George II) has any memorial.

Until the Dissolution of the Monastery burial within the Abbey Church was almost entirely confined to Sovereigns, members of the Royal Family, a few royal favourites and some of the Abbots. In the second half of the 16th century, however, stately monuments to some of the great Elizabethans began to be erected in the Abbey, and throughout the 17th and 18th centuries memorials to statesmen, lawyers, soldiers, sailors, writers, poets and musicians, and to many who had little or no claim to be thus commemorated, began to crowd the walls. We may deplore the result and even more the ruthless mutilation which took place in fixing them in place, but it must be remembered that many of these tablets and monuments are of considerable artistic value, and that nowhere else can there be found so remarkable a sequence of memorials from medieval times to the present day. Moreover in their own way these memorials have contributed to give the Abbey its nation-wide character. It is only within the last hundred years or so that burial within the Abbey, or erection of a tablet there, has come once again to be regarded as a mark of special distinction.

At the same time there began to grow up a new conception of what the Abbey might come to mean in the life of the nation. Under Dean Stanley and his successors it became much more of a national church than it had ever been before. The building itself, too, began to be studied not as a museum of antiquities but as an incomparable whole of inexhaustible interest. Broadcasting and television have made known its history and the beauty of its services, so that in a very real sense it has become 'the parish church of the English-speaking peoples' and 'belonging to no diocese, it belongs to all'.

William Ewart Gladstone.

Sir Walter Scott.

Dr. Samuel Johnson.

Opposite: King Richard II. This painting hangs inside the West door of Westminster Abbey.

The Constitution

W. R. J. Pullen, LL.B., F.C.I.S. Chapter Clerk

Westminster Abbey, or the Collegiate Church of St. Peter in Westminster to give the legal title, is a Royal Peculiar. The Sovereign is the Visitor and the Abbey is not subject to the jurisdiction of the Bishop of the Diocese or indeed of the Archbishop of the Province.

The present constitution stems from a Royal Charter of Queen Elizabeth I dated 21 May 1560. A set of draft statutes was drawn up by Dean Bill, the first Dean of the Collegiate Church. These statutes were, however, never signed. Whether this was intentional or accidental is not known. But time has proved the omission to be fortunate in that it has enabled the Abbey constitution to be flexible and to be varied with the times. Certain specific questions relating to the Constitution were submitted by the Canons to the Royal Visitor in 1911 and referred by the King to the Lord Chancellor for his advice. As a result, it was established that the statutes had no legal authority and that the Abbey was governed by Charter, Royal Letters and Custom, but that, where the custom was neither clear nor continuous, the statutes could be referred to as evidence of what the ancient custom presumably was. Charters, Royal Letters (or Statutes if they are signed) can only be altered by the proper external authority. Customs, however, all the world over, have a way of altering themselves and Abbey customs are no exception. The Minutes of the Dean and Chapter over the years record many such changes by formal resolutions of Chapter.

Since 1560 there have been two Supplemental Charters: the first in 1951, abolished freehold tenure of office for Minor Canons and Lay Officers appointed after the grant of the Charter, and the second in 1958 gave the Dean and Chapter wider powers of investment for their corporate funds, enabling them to invest in equities.

Royal Letters were issued in 1667, 1746, 1836 and 1868 dealing with the allocation of official houses, residence and attendance at Services by the Dean and Canons, the quorum for Chapter Meetings and the Sub-Dean's authority to call Chapter Meetings when the Dean cannot be present.

The Chapter Minutes provide the usual source of information and authority for the various customs which have now been incorporated into the Constitution because of usage over a long period. For example, it would be unthinkable for the procedure to be varied whereby the Dean and Chapter, as a Corporate Body, receive the Sovereign when she visits the Abbey. Likewise it is customary for the Canons of Westminster to be present in Henry VII's Chapel during installation ceremonies of the Order of the Bath, even though they are not members of the Order.

The Dean and Canons of Westminster (not of Westminster Abbey as they are sometimes mistakenly called) are appointed by the Sovereign, in practice on the advice of the Prime Minister, and form a Body Corporate known as the Dean and Chapter. They are corporately responsible for the government of the Abbey and for its fabric and finances. The Dean presides at Chapter Meetings which are held every fortnight to deal with the business of the Abbey, in rather the same way as a Board of Directors of a Company. The Dean is personally responsible for the order and form of the Services. In ecclesiastical terms he is 'The Ordinary'. This explains why the words 'By Order of the Dean' appear on the posters giving details of Abbey Services. The Dean, as The Ordinary, has complete authority to decide who shall be baptised, married, buried or commemorated in the Abbey. He is required to be in residence for a specified period every year and to preach on certain days, including Christmas Day and Easter Day.

There are at present four Canons. They are required to keep months of residence and as Canons-in-Residence to be responsible for duties at Statutory Services. The Canons also hold additional appointments of Sub-Dean, Archdeacon, Treasurer, Steward and Lector Theologiae. Appointments to these offices are made annually. The Sub-Dean is appointed by the Dean as his personal deputy to act for him when he is 'ill or absent in foreign parts'. Appointment to the other offices is in the hands of the Dean and Chapter. The Archdeacon in recent years has had special responsibilities for the livings of which the Dean and

The Great Seal of Westminster Abbey

Chapter are Patrons. The Treasurer (with the Receiver-General) is responsible for the finances and investments. The Steward is in charge of the College Garden and Precincts and is the Chapter's Guest-Master and arranges all official hospitality. It is the duty of the Lector Theologiae to promote religious teaching by means of lectures.

The Dean and Chapter are assisted by the Minor Canons and Lay Officers of the Collegiate Body. These officers (both clerical and lay) are appointed by the Dean on terms and conditions laid down by the Dean and Chapter. The maxim is 'The Dean appoints; the Chapter pay'. Since 1951, they are all appointed on service agreements.

The constitution of the Abbey, like the constitution of our country itself, is not written down in one document but is based largely on custom. This has enabled successive Deans and Chapters in their wisdom to direct the affairs of the Abbey with a comparatively free hand preserving its peculiar status and enabling it to perform a continuing function as the central shrine of the British Commonwealth.

The Benefices

To keep up a vast building such as Westminster Abbey has always been a costly business. To enable the monks to do this, and also to maintain their life of worship, study and toil, this monastic foundation was endowed with lands throughout the country. There were no Westminster Abbey Appeals in those days, though money did come in from the offertories of pilgrims at the Shrine of St. Edward! The estates, however, were surrendered to the Ecclesiastical Commissioners in 1865 for an annual money payment. The link with these days is preserved through the advowsons of the livings which the Abbey still holds. The following parishes are in its gift:–

PARISH	*Date of Advowson*	*Incumbent*
Diocese of London		
St. Bartholomew the Great, Smithfield	1951	N. E. Wallbank, M.A., Ph.D., Mus.D.
St. Bride, Fleet Street	1308	Dewi Morgan, B.A.
Holy Trinity, Kensington Gore, with All Saints, Kensington	1849	D. W. Cleverley Ford, B.D., M.Th.
St. James the Less, Westminster	1862	Vacant (Priest-in-Charge: G. C. Moore, A.K.C.)
St. Matthew, Westminster	1851	Ronald Royle, A.K.C., M.C.
St. Peter, Belsize Park,	1859	P. L. Brock, M.B.E., M.A.
Diocese of Chelmsford		
Canewdon with Paglesham, Essex	1879	N. J. Kelly, B.D., A.K.C.
Maldon St. Mary, Essex	1502	G. L. Child
South Benfleet, Essex	1086	A. G. Banks, B.D., A.K.C.
Diocese of Ely		
Alconbury with Weston, Huntingdon	1542	G. F. Davies
Bassingbourne, Cambridgeshire	1502	C. Prior, A.K.C.
Godmanchester, Huntingdon	1542	N. Munt, A.K.C.
Diocese of Hereford		
Mathon, Worcestershire	1542	L. H. S. Bagshaw, M.B.E., A.K.C.
Diocese of Oxford		
Chaddleworth with Fawley, Berkshire	1531	E. Harding, L.Th., Hon.C.F.
Islip with Noke, Oxford	1203	A. W. Blanchett
Stanford-in-the-Vale, with Goosey and Hatford, Berkshire	1500	H. S. Fry, O.B.E., M.A.
Steventon, Berkshire	1399	G. W. Bowker, T.D., M.A.
Turweston with Westbury, Buckinghamshire	1292	R. E. Frank, B.Sc. (Econ).
Diocese of Rochester		
Otford, Kent	1548	F. C. Bunch, M.A.
Shoreham, Kent	1548	D. E. Benbow, M.A.
Diocese of Worcester		
Castle Morton, Worcestershire	1571	G. T. Haigh, M.A., M.Litt., L.Th.
Defford with Besford, Worcestershire	1557	P. D. Chippendale, B.A.
Eckington, Worcestershire	1557	Vacant
Longdon, Worcestershire	1571	L. Davies
Pershore with Pinvin and Wick, Worcestershire	1557	P. C. Moore, M.A., D.Phil.
West Malvern, Worcestershire	1841	N. S. P. Baron, M.A.

The Abbey Flags

The Royal Standard is flown whenever the Sovereign is within the Abbey Precinct, also when the Sovereign opens Parliament (a privilege granted by King Edward VII).

The Flag of St. Peter is flown on all Church Festivals.

The Abbey Flag is flown on occasions of domestic significance; for instance, on days associated with St. Edward the Confessor, Westminster School Election, Feast of the Dedication. It is also flown on Royal Birthdays.

The Union Flag is flown on Commonwealth Day and Remembrance Sunday: and on the appropriate days the flags of the National Saints, St. George (April 23), St. Andrew (November 30), St. David (March 1) and St. Patrick (March 17).

The Dominion Flags are flown on their respective Foundation Days, viz. Australia (January 26), New Zealand (February 6), Canada (July 1): the Royal Air Force Flag, on the Commemoration of the Battle of Britain.

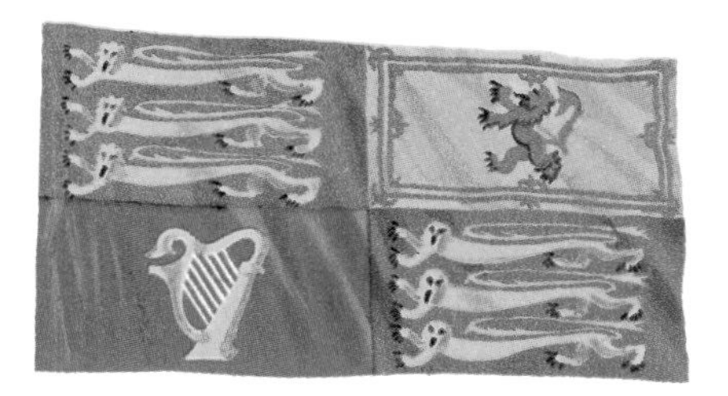

The Royal Standard.

The Flag of St. Peter.

The Abbey Flag

The Abbey Bells

There are eight bells. Half an hour before Matins and Evensong the Sixth and Seventh bells are chimed for five minutes, and if a sermon is to be preached this chiming is followed by forty strokes on the Tenor bell. A quarter of an hour before the service the Fifth bell is chimed for ten minutes followed by the Treble bell for five minutes. Before the early Celebrations of Holy Communion on weekdays a small bell is rung for five minutes.

On the occasion of the death of a member of the College the Sixth bell is tolled every half minute for half an hour; on the death of the Dean or a member of the Royal Family the Tenor bell is tolled every minute for an hour.

After a Funeral or Memorial Service a half-muffled peal is rung.

RINGING DAYS

Ringing on eight bells takes place on the following days, generally between the hours of 12 noon and 1 p.m.:

1966

New Year's Day (Jan. 1)
The Epiphany (Jan. 6)
The Purification (Feb. 2)
Accession Day (Feb. 6)
St. Benedict's Day (Mar. 21)
Easter Day (April 10)
St. George's Day (April 23)
Ascension Day (May 19)
Commonwealth Day (May 24)
Election of the Mayor of Westminster (May 26)
Whit-Sunday (May 29)
Coronation Day (June 2)
Official Celebration of the Queen's Birthday (June 11)
St. Peter's Day (June 29)
Election Sunday (July 24)
The reopening of the Law Courts, when the Lord Chancellor, the Judges and the Members of the Bar attend a special service (Oct. 3)
Translation of St. Edward the King and Confessor (Oct 13)
All Saints' Day (Nov. 1)
Remembrance Sunday (Nov. 13)
Foundation Day, Anniversary of the Accession of Queen Elizabeth I (Nov. 17)
Wedding Day of Her Majesty Queen Elizabeth II (Nov. 20)
Christmas Day (Dec. 25)
St. Stephen's Day (Dec. 26)
Holy Innocents' Day (Dec. 28)

The Union Flag.

The Flag of St. George.

The Flag of Canada.

The Flag of Australia.

The Flag of New Zealand.

PROGRAMME
of special services
and events
to celebrate the
900th Year of
WESTMINSTER ABBEY
A Canon of 4 parts in One
By Dr John Blow

REGULAR SERVICES

SUNDAYS

8 a.m.	Holy Communion
10.30 a.m.	Matins and Sermon
11.30 a.m.	Holy Communion (This Service is sung on Festivals and on the second and fourth Sunday in each month)
3 p.m.	Evensong and Sermon
6.30 p.m.	Congregational Service and Sermon in The Nave

WEEKDAYS

7.30 a.m.	Said Matins
8.00 a.m.	Holy Communion
9.00 a.m.	Westminster School Service (In Term Time only)
12.30 p.m.	Holy Communion (Fridays) and
12.30 p.m.	Lunchtime Service (Wednesdays) both in St Margaret's Church, April to September
5.00 p.m.	Evensong (3 p.m. Saturdays and Bank Holidays)

HOURS OF OPENING AND CLOSING OF THE ABBEY IN 1966

The Abbey is opened daily throughout the year at 8 a.m.

CLOSING TIMES

January 1 to March 31 and October 1 to December 28	6.00 p.m., with the exception of WEDNESDAYS when the Abbey will remain open until 9 p.m.

April 1 to September 30	Mondays, Tuesdays, Thursdays, Saturdays, Sundays	8.00 p.m.
	Wednesdays	9.00 p.m.
	Fridays	6.00 p.m.

NOTE: The above times are subject to alteration if made necessary by such events as Special Services.

THE ABBEY BELLS

On 28 December, 1965, Holy Innocents' Day, there will be a full peal of bells rung to inaugurate the Abbey's Nongentenary Year, and a full peal on Holy Innocents' Day 1966 to close the Year. These full peals will be rung by the Abbey's own band of Ringers.

To mark the three Special Days in 1966, St Benedict's Day 21 March; St Peter's Day 29 June; and St Edward's Day 13 October there will be a quarter peal rung by the Ringers of The Ancient Society of College Youths, The Society of Royal Cumberland Youths, and the Middlesex County Association and London Diocesan Guild Change Ringers respectively.

EXHIBITIONS

The ONE PEOPLE Exhibition in The Chapter House and the ABBEY TREASURES Exhibition in The Norman Undercroft will be open to the public after their official openings on 4 January and 10 January 1966 respectively, during the following times throughout the year.

Monday, Tuesday, Thursday, Friday, Saturday	9.30 a.m. to 5.00 p.m.
Wednesday	9.30 a.m. to 9.00 p.m.

There will be a Science Exhibition, sponsored by The Royal Society and The British Association, during August.

An Exhibition of Coins in The Pyx Chapel will open on June 3 and will be followed in September by an Exhibition sponsored by The Council of Christians and Jews.

POETRY READINGS:

During June and July there will be programmes of Poetry and Prose readings with music every Friday between 1 and 2 p.m. The programmes will be designed so as to illuminate various themes and will represent the works of writers who are either buried or have memorials in the Abbey.

Amongst those who hope to take part in these programmes are:

Dame Edith Evans
Dame Sybil Thorndyke
Sir Lewis Casson
Mr Andrew Cruickshank
Miss Vanessa Redgrave
Sir Michael Redgrave
Mr Cecil Day-Lewis
Professor Nevill Coghill

ORGAN RECITALS

Tickets for all Organ Recitals available from the Chapter Office, Westminster Abbey, SW1, price 5/-.

Day and date	Time	Service or event
		DECEMBER 1965
HOLY INNOCENTS DAY Tuesday 28	7.00 a.m.	Said Matins
	7.30 a.m.	Holy Communion (High Altar)
	8.30 a.m.	Hoisting of the Abbey Flag
	11.00 a.m.	INAUGURAL SERVICE (attended by H.M. The Queen and other members of the Royal Family) Preacher: The Dean
	3.00 p.m.	CAROL SERVICE
	4.15 p.m.	Switching on of the floodlighting of the Abbey by the Mayor of Westminster (a full peal of bells will be rung by the Abbey Band of Ringers (3¼ hrs))
Note: On this Inaugural Day the Abbey will remain open until 10.00 p.m.		
Thursday 30	12 noon	Commemoration of the Centenary of the birth of Rudyard Kipling with Wreath Laying in Poets' Corner Readings by Michael Hordern from Kipling's works
Friday 31	11.45 p.m.	New Year's Eve WATCH NIGHT SERVICE
		JANUARY 1966
Saturday 1	3.00 p.m.	WESTMINSTER ABBEY OLD CHORISTERS' ASSOCIATION Festal Evensong
Sunday 2	3.00 p.m.	Orchestral Concert presented by the B.B.C., direct broadcast on Third Programme
Tuesday 4	11.30 a.m.	Opening of the 'ONE PEOPLE' Exhibition in The Chapter House
Thursday 6	6.30 p.m.	EPIPHANY SERVICE with symbolic exchange of gifts
Note: During the Abbey Choir Holiday – Friday January 7 to Evensong Saturday January 15 – the weekday services will be plain. The Services on Sunday January 9 will be sung by The Ambrosian Singers		
Monday 10	11.30 a.m.	Opening of the Exhibition of ABBEY TREASURES in the Norman Undercroft by H.R.H. The Princess Margaret, Countess of Snowdon
Friday 14	11.15 a.m.	WESTMINSTER HOSPITAL 250th ANNIVERSARY SERVICE. Preacher: The Dean
Tuesday 18	10.30 a.m.	WESTMINSTER SCHOOL OPENING OF TERM SERVICE
Tuesday 18 to Tuesday 25		WEEK OF PRAYER FOR CHRISTIAN UNITY Interdenominational addresses after Evensong Address given by :– Tuesday 18 The Rt. Rev. Ralph Dean (Anglican) Wednesday 19 The Most Reverend Antony, Archbishop of Sourozh (Russian Orthodox) Thursday 20 The Rev. John Weller (British Council of Churches) Friday 21 The Rev. Father T. Corbishley. S.J. (Roman Catholic) Saturday 22 The Rev. Dr. Maurice Barnett, Westminster Central Hall (Methodist) Monday 24 The Rev. Kenneth Slack, St. Andrew's Church, Cheam (Presbyterian) Tuesday 25 The Rev. Dr. E. A. Payne, Baptist Church, Southampton Row (Baptist)
Sunday 23	4.00 p.m.	SERVICE AFTER TRAFALGAR SQUARE UNITY RALLY Preacher: The Dean
		FEBRUARY 1966
Wednesday 2	4.00 p.m.	EVENSONG – Broadcast on B.B.C. Home Service
Monday 7	1.30 p.m.	Centenary of the Organized Women's Movement – Wreath Laying on Memorial to Dame Millicent Fawcett
Wednesday 9	4.00 p.m.	EVENSONG – Broadcast on B.B.C. Home Service
Saturday 19	11.00 a.m.	SERVICE FOR BOY SCOUTS AND GIRL GUIDES – Wreath Laying on Memorial to Lord Baden-Powell
ASH WEDNESDAY Wednesday 23	5.00 p.m.	EVENSONG – Sermon in Commemoration of Dame Grace Gethin followed by distribution of the Dean's Gift Preacher: The Ven. Archdeacon E. F. Carpenter

Day and date	Time	Service or event
		MARCH 1966
Tuesday 1	5.45 p.m.	LENT LECTURE by The Dean, introducing the series 'Contemporary Christian Concerns'
Tuesday 8	5.45 p.m.	LENT LECTURE by the Rt. Rev. Joost de Blank Subject: 'Christianity in Modern Urban Society'
Wednesday 9	6.00 p.m.	LONDON UNIVERSITY PRESENTATION DAY SERVICE (attended by H.M. Queen Elizabeth, The Queen Mother) Preacher: The Rev. Professor C. F. Evans, New Testament Professor of the University of London
Thursday 10	7.00 p.m.	Recital by the combined choirs of Magdalen and New College, Oxford
Monday 14	11.15 a.m.	WESTMINSTER SCHOOL CONFIRMATION SERVICE
Tuesday 15	5.45 p.m.	LENT LECTURE by The Ven. Archdeacon E. F. Carpenter Subject: 'Christianity and Cosmology'
Sunday 20	3.00 p.m.	MOTHERING SUNDAY – SPECIAL FAMILY SERVICE
ST BENEDICT'S DAY Monday 21	11.30 a.m.	SERVICE FOR MEMBERS OF BENEDICTINE COMMUNITIES IN THE UNITED KINGDOM AND OVERSEAS
Tuesday 22	5.45 p.m.	LENT LECTURE by Canon M. S. Stancliffe Subject: 'Nature, Faith and Sacrament'
Wednesday 23	11.30 a.m.	Unveiling of the Colonial Services Memorial by H.M. The Queen
Saturday 26	11.00 a.m.	SERVICE FOR POLICE, PRISON, PROBATION, AND AFTERCARE SERVICES (Metropolitan Police Band and Choir)
Monday 28	7.00 p.m.	Bach's 'ST MATTHEW PASSION' sung by Westminster Abbey Choir and Westminster Abbey Special Choir (No tickets required)
Tuesday 29	5.45 p.m.	LENT LECTURE by Canon M. A. C. Warren Subject: 'The Relationship between Christianity and Other World Religions'
		APRIL 1966
Saturday 2	6.00 p.m.	BISHOP OF LONDON'S ADULT CONFIRMATION SERVICE
Monday 4 Tuesday 5 Wednesday 6	12.30 p.m.	Holy Week addresses by the Rt. Rev. Ambrose Reeves, formerly Bishop of Johannesburg
Tuesday 5	5.45 p.m.	LENT LECTURE by The Dean. Subject: 'Faith and Devotion'
MAUNDY THURSDAY Thursday 7	11.30 a.m. 5.15 p.m. 6.00 p.m.	Distribution of the Royal Maundy by H.M. The Queen Said EVENSONG HOLY COMMUNION
EASTER SUNDAY Sunday 10	 6.45 p.m. to 7.30 p.m.	USUAL SUNDAY SERVICES B.B.C. SONGS OF PRAISE T.V. Transmission
EASTER MONDAY Monday 11	3.00 p.m.	EASTER CAROL SERVICE NOTE: From April 15 until May 1 Services will be sung by the Choir of WASHINGTON CATHEDRAL, U.S.A.
Sunday 17	10.30 a.m.	SERVICE FOR AMERICANS IN LONDON Lesson to be read by His Excellency the American Ambassador
Monday 18	11.30 a.m.	SERVICE FOR THE INTERNATIONAL CONVENTION OF VARIETY CLUBS Preacher: The Rt. Rev. Cuthbert Bardsley, Bishop of Coventry
Friday 22	2.30 p.m.	SERVICE FOR THE ARMED FORCES OF THE CROWN Preacher: The Rt. Rev. Victor Pike, Bishop of Sherborne (former Chaplain General)
Monday 25	12 noon	ANZAC DAY SPECIAL SERVICE
Wednesday 27	4.00 p.m.	EVENSONG – Sung by the Choir of WASHINGTON CATHEDRAL and broadcast on the B.B.C. Home Service
Friday 29	2.30 p.m.	SERVICE FOR SCHOOLS IN WESTMINSTER Preacher: The Rev. John Williams of S.P.C.K.

Day and date	Time	Service or event
		MAY 1966
Tuesday 3	6.15 p.m.	Organ Recital by Jeanne de Messieux (France)
Thursday 5	8.00 a.m.	HOLY COMMUNION attended by members of the Church Army
Sunday 8	8.00 p.m.	Organ Recital by Simon Preston
Monday 9 to Saturday 14		WEEK OF 'HOMAGE TO MUSIC' (Patron H.M. Queen Elizabeth the Queen Mother)
	8.00 p.m.	Monday: London Symphony Orchestra, Ambrosian Singers and Soloists
	5.30 p.m.	Tuesday: Amadeus Quartet with Gervaise de Peyer
	8.00 p.m.	The Bach Choir
	8.00 p.m.	Wednesday: London Symphony Orchestra, Ambrosian Singers and Soloists
	8.00 p.m.	Thursday: London Symphony Orchestra, Ambrosian Singers and Soloists
	8.00 p.m.	Friday: English Chamber Orchestra, Schütz Choir and Soloists
	8.00 p.m.	Saturday: B.B.C. Symphony Orchestra, Chorus and Choral Society (Broadcast B.B.C. Third Programme)
Thursday 12	12.15 p.m.	Presentation by Trinity Church New York of plaque in memory of King William III and Queen Anne
Saturday 14	12 noon and 2.30 p.m.	Performances by the Westminster Morris Dancers in the Precincts
Tuesday 17	6.30 p.m.	National Florence Nightingale Memorial Service and Ceremony of the Lamp. Preacher: The Rt. Rev. G. A. Ellison, Bishop of Chester
Friday 20		SERVICE FOR THE PRESS (Provisional date)
Wednesday 25 to		FESTIVAL OF FLOWERS organised by the National Association of Flower Arrangement Societies (Provisional)
Friday 27	11.30 a.m.	Friday: NATIONAL FLOWER SERVICE (Provisional)
WHITSUNDAY Sunday 29	3.00 p.m.	SERVICE OF INTERNATIONAL CHRISTIAN WITNESS Preacher: The Archbishop of Canterbury
		JUNE 1966
Thursday 2	12.45 p.m.	Unveiling of Memorial to Caedmon
	7.00 p.m.	CIVIC SERVICE (attended by the Mayor, Aldermen and Councillors of Westminster in Civic State)
Friday 3	11.00 a.m.	Opening of Exhibition of Coins in the Pyx Chapel
	1–2 p.m.	Readings in Poets' Corner
Monday 6	5.45 p.m.	First of series of Trinity Lectures entitled 'The Medieval Abbey' given by The Rev. J. C. Dickinson, B.A., B.Litt., F.S.A., F.R.Hist.S., Lecturer in Theology, Birmingham University Subject: 'The Place of Kings'
Tuesday 7	6.15 p.m.	Organ Recital by Fernando Germani (Italy)
Wednesday 8	6.30 p.m.	Annual Commemoration and Wreath Laying on the grave of Charles Dickens
Thursday 9	8.00 p.m.	Concert by students of the Royal College of Music
Friday 10	1–2 p.m.	Readings in Poets' Corner
Monday 13	5.45 p.m.	Second Trinity Lecture by The Rev. J. C. Dickinson Subject: 'The House of God'
Friday 17	1–2 p.m.	Readings in Poets' Corner
Monday 20	5.45 p.m.	Third Trinity Lecture given by The Rev. J. C. Dickinson Subject: 'The Problem of Society'
Friday 24	1–2 p.m.	Readings in Poets' Corner
Saturday 25	3.00 p.m.	Evensong sung by combined choirs from Abbey Benefices
ST PETER'S DAY Wednesday 29	a.m.	SERVICE FOR CHURCH AND STATE
	6.00 p.m.	CHORAL EUCHARIST attended by Incumbents and Parishioners of the Deaneries of Westminster, Paddington and St Marylebone
		JULY 1966
Friday 1	1–2 p.m.	Readings in Poets' Corner
Sunday 3	3.00 p.m.	Ecumenical Service of Dedication for the Ministry to Mariners
Monday 4	7.00 p.m.	FESTAL EVENSONG sung by The Westminster Abbey Choir and The Westminster Abbey Special Choir (No tickets required)

Day and date	Time	Service or event
Tuesday 5	6.15 p.m.	Organ Recital by Anton Heiller (Austria)
Wednesday 6	12.30–2 p.m.	Concert by the Central Band of the Royal Air Force in College Garden
Friday 8	1–2 p.m.	Readings in Poets' Corner
Wednesday 13	12.30–2 p.m.	Concert by the Chatham Band of the Royal Engineers in College Garden
	6.30 p.m.	Recital by combined choirs of King's and St John's Colleges Cambridge
Friday 15	1–2 p.m.	Readings in Poets' Corner
Tuesday 19 Wednesday 20 Thursday 21 Friday 22 Saturday 23		WESTMINSTER ABBEY MARKET AND FAIR IN DEAN'S YARD (Patron: H.R.H. Princess Alexandra, the Hon. Mrs Angus Ogilvy)
Wednesday 20	12.30–2 p.m.	Concert by the Band of the Irish Guards in Dean's Yard
	7.30 p.m.	GREY COAT HOSPITAL FOUNDATION SERVICE
Friday 22	1–2 p.m.	Readings in Poets' Corner
Wednesday 27	12.30–2 p.m.	Concert by the Band of the Portsmouth Group Royal Marines in College Garden
Friday 29	1–2 p.m.	Readings in Poets' Corner

AUGUST 1966

Day and date	Time	Service or event
Tuesday 2	6.15 p.m.	Organ Recital by George Thalben-Ball (London)
Wednesday 3	12.30–2 p.m.	Concert by the Metropolitan Police Band in College Garden
Wednesday 10	12.30–2 p.m.	Concert by a Band of the Household Brigade in College Garden
Wednesday 17	12.30–2 p.m.	Concert by a Band of the Household Brigade in College Garden
Wednesday 24	12.30–2 p.m.	Concert by a Band of the Household Brigade in College Garden
Wednesday 31	12.30–2 p.m.	Concert by a Band of the Household Brigade in College Garden

The Abbey Choir will be on Holiday from August 4 to September 17 (Choristers) and until September 1 (Lay-Vicars). Services from August 4 to 31 will be sung by The Royal School of Church Music, Summer Course. Services sung by men only from September 1 to September 17.

SEPTEMBER 1966

Day and date	Time	Service or event
Tuesday 6	6.15 p.m.	Organ Recital by Gillian Weir (London)
Wednesday 7	12.30–2 p.m.	Concert by the Band of the Royal Electrical and Mechanical Engineers in College Garden
Wednesday 14	12.30–2 p.m.	Concert by the Band of the Royal Corps of Signals in College Garden
Sunday 18		Service of Thanksgiving for Victory gained in the Battle of Britain in September 1940
Wednesday 21	12.30–2 p.m.	Concert by the Band of the Portsmouth Group Royal Marines in College Garden
	8.00 p.m.	Performance of the Monteverdi 'VESPERS', in aid of the Historic Churches Preservation Trust. Application for tickets to the Secretary, Historic Churches Trust, Fulham Palace, SW6
Saturday 24	3.00 p.m.	Festal Evensong attended by National Federation of Old Choristers' Associations
Wednesday 28	12.30–2 p.m.	Concert by the Central Band of the Royal Air Force in College Garden

OCTOBER 1966

Day and date	Time	Service or event
Monday 3	11.45 a.m.	SERVICE attended by the Lord Chancellor, Judges, and Members of the Legal Profession (in robes)
Tuesday 4	6.15 p.m.	Organ Recital by Marilyn Mason (U.S.A.)
Sunday 9	3.00 p.m.	SERVICE FOR VOLUNTARY ORGANISATIONS WORKING IN THE INTERNATIONAL FIELD
Wednesday 12		Abbey closed at 6 p.m. for rehearsal
ST EDWARD'S DAY Thursday 13	7.30 p.m.	LITURGICAL PERFORMANCE OF BEETHOVEN'S 'MISSA SOLEMNIS'

Day and date	Time	Service or event
Saturday 15	2.00 p.m.	Westminster and Berkshire Dragoons PARADE SERVICE
Tuesday 18	11.30 a.m.	SERVICE FOR SCIENCE AND TECHNOLOGY
Monday 24	11.30 a.m.	SERVICE ON THE OCCASION OF THE 21st ANNIVERSARY OF THE UNITED NATIONS
Saturday 29	3.00 p.m.	NATIONAL HARVEST FESTIVAL THANKSGIVING SERVICE
		NOVEMBER 1966
Tuesday 1	6.15 p.m.	Organ Recital by Robert Baker (U.S.A.)
Tuesday 8	8.00 a.m.	Celebration of the Holy Communion. Special invitation to Bishops attending Church Assembly
Sunday 13	10.30 a.m.	REMEMBRANCE SUNDAY SERVICE
ST ANDREW'S DAY Wednesday 30	6.30 p.m.	MISSIONARY SERVICE
		DECEMBER 1966
Thursday 1	8.00 p.m.	Concert by students of The Royal Academy of Music
Monday 5	7.00 p.m.	CHORAL AND ORCHESTRAL CONCERT by The Westminster Abbey Choir and Westminster Abbey Special Choir (No tickets required)
Tuesday 6	6.15 p.m.	Organ Recital by Francis Jackson (York)
Wednesday 7	12.30 p.m.	Advent Lecture by The Dean. Subject: 'Forward from 1966'
Saturday 10	12–1 p.m.	DECLARATION OF HUMAN RIGHTS DAY An invitation will be extended by the Dean and Chapter of Westminster to members of all great Faiths of the world to join in a Service of Silence
Wednesday 14	12.30 p.m.	Advent Lecture by The Dean
Saturday 17	12 noon	Annual Commemoration and Wreath Laying on Memorial to Dr. Samuel Johnson
Wednesday 21	12.30 p.m.	Advent Lecture by The Dean
Sunday 25 Monday 26 Tuesday 27		Usual Christmas Services
Wednesday 28	11.00 a.m.	SPECIAL CLOSING SERVICE

THE ST EDWARD PLATE

The Dean and Chapter have commissioned the Spode China Factory to produce a numbered limited issue of 900 St Edward Plates. With the approval of H.M. The Queen, these plates will bear the Royal Coat of Arms. They will be on sale by application to the Receiver-General, Westminster Abbey at a cost of £10.10.0. Each Plate will be packed in a presentation box containing a certificate personally signed by The Dean of Westminster.

THE WESTMINSTER ABBEY PLATE

The Westminster Abbey Plate, also designed and produced by Spode, bears the Great Seal of the Abbey in gold leaf. This plate will be on sale in the Abbey Bookshop and throughout the country, in a presentation box at £5.5.0.

COMMEMORATIVE BOOK

There will be 900 specially bound copies of this book, personally signed by The Dean of Westminster, obtainable from the Abbey Bookshop and Westerham Press at £15.15.0 each.

COMMEMORATIVE MEDALS

A medal to commemorate the 900th Anniversary of Westminster Abbey has been commissioned by the Dean and Chapter. This has been designed by Mr Michael Rizzello and struck by the Royal Mint. The medals will be on sale in the Abbey Bookshop and through Spink and Sons.

The $2\frac{1}{4}$ inch medal will be struck in 22 carat gold at £100, Silver at £5, Bronze at £2.10.0.

A set of all three medals is also available in a presentation case at £110.

The gold medals will be limited to an issue of 900 and will be numbered; each medal will be sold with a certificate personally signed by The Dean of Westminster.

HOUSE OF KINGS

This is the title of the full illustrated history of the Abbey to be published in June 1966 by John Baker Ltd. It will be edited by the Ven. Archdeacon Edward Carpenter, and consists of 10 sections each by a specialist in his own subject or period. Obtainable from the Abbey Bookshop and all booksellers. Price £3. 3. 0.

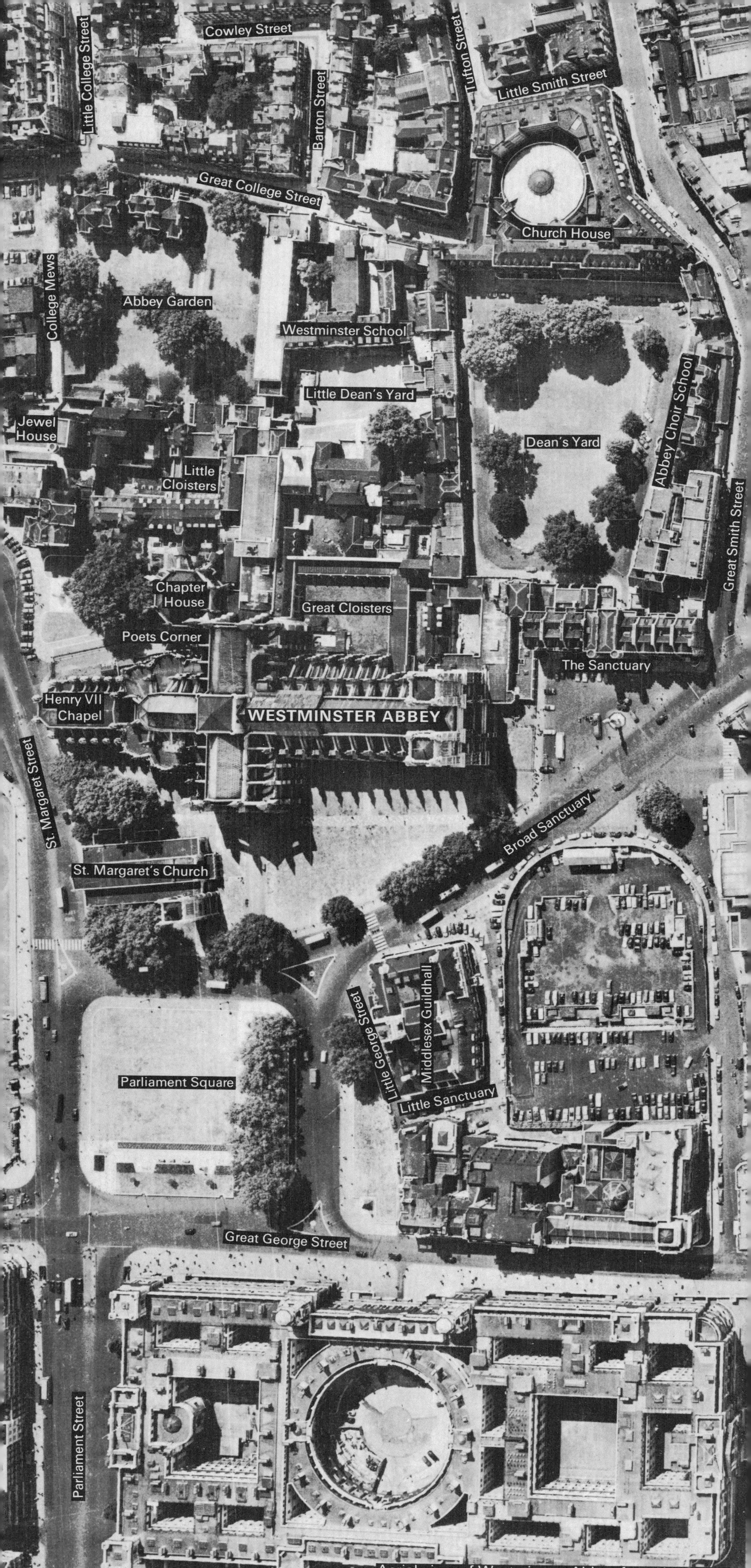

Cowley Street
Little College Street
Tufton Street
Little Smith Street
Barton Street
Great College Street
Church House
College Mews
Abbey Garden
Westminster School
Little Dean's Yard
Jewel House
Dean's Yard
Abbey Choir School
Little Cloisters
Great Smith Street
Chapter House
Great Cloisters
Poets Corner
The Sanctuary
Henry VII Chapel
WESTMINSTER ABBEY
St. Margaret Street
Broad Sanctuary
St. Margaret's Church
Little George Street
Middlesex Guildhall
Parliament Square
Little Sanctuary
Great George Street
Parliament Street

Aerial view of Westminster Abbey from the South

The Architecture

S. E. Dykes Bower, M.A., F.R.I.B.A., F.S.A.
Surveyor of the Fabric

Among the great Gothic churches of England, Westminster Abbey has always been unique. More closely identified with the national life than any other, it has been, architecturally, the least insular in outlook. From the time that Edward the Confessor founded it as a Benedictine monastery and built the first Abbey Church in the Norman style before the Norman conquest, European influences have moulded its development and differentiated it in aspect from other contemporary work.

Henry III, to whom credit must be given for the present Abbey Church, was more than an architectural enthusiast; familiarity with what for him was not foreign territory enlarged his vision and stimulated his ideas. The work that was going on in France could hardly have failed to do so, for the galaxy of cathedrals that were rising in incomparable splendour – Amiens, Rheims, Chartres, Bourges, and many others – far surpassed in constructional daring anything that had been attempted in England and spoke almost a new architectural language. They fired his ambition as much as his admiration: and no doubt it was a desire to achieve something similar that partly determined him to mark the canonization of Edward the Confessor by building a new and more glorious church to enshrine the royal saint.

Without his inspiration it is unlikely that Westminster Abbey would be what it is – in plan and proportions more French than English, and yet not wholly one or the other. For if the conception owes much to France, its execution is clearly English. The king seems not to have brought over a French architect to design it, but to have sent an Englishman to study and absorb all he could see and then produce a native equivalent. The result is a remarkable testimony to the wisdom of this procedure: for if in virtuosity Westminster is in some respects outclassed, in beauty it is inferior to none. Lofty by English standards, it rivals neither the height nor the complexity of plan of its French relations: but its interior avoids a tendency to overdramatic exaggeration, as at Beauvais, and the treatment of the apse – always a difficult architectural problem – is managed more skilfully than in many French cathedrals where the bay division is too crowded and the arches have to be stilted.

In purity of design and quality of detail Henry III's work at Westminster reaches a high level of perfection; and perhaps the greatest tribute that could be paid to it was that, when the building of the nave commenced a hundred years after his death, Edward III's architect, Henry Yevele, refrained from any fundamental change. So far from seizing the opportunity to build in the latest fashion of his time, he contrived that between the old and the new there should be no perceptible break. Their integration into one harmonious whole is due to this act of self-abnegation and artistic judgement by which a fine architect, in honouring another, unwittingly did honour to himself.

How much stylistic change was taking place at the time can be appreciated by recalling that Henry VII's chapel was started before the nave was finished. Here again royal munificence, as well as discernment over the choice of architect, enriched the Abbey with a masterpiece that outshines other works of its kind in England. The splendour of this sumptuous chapel is to be found not only in the technical feats of its construction, but in its combination of bold design, refined detail and sculptural adornment. It is opulent but not vulgar, lavish in ornament without a trace of coarseness. The end of the medieval epoch could not have culminated in anything nobler.

The last structural addition, completing the building as we know it, was the raising of the two west towers. A liking for these may be, to some extent, an acquired taste. But what is interesting is that Hawksmoor, the most classical of architects, felt the Gothic magnetism of the Abbey and recognised the demands it made. If there are anomalies in his design, its vigour more than atones for them and few would now wish to see the west front different from what it is.

The architectural interest of the Abbey, however, embraces much more than its structure. From the earliest years when a burial place as near as possible to the Shrine of the Confessor was the privilege sought by kings and nobles alike, tombs, monuments and memorials of every kind have multiplied within its walls. If there is cause to regret their number and the injury some have inflicted upon the architecture, the merits of many of those dating from the 16th, 17th and 18th centuries fully entitle them to the space they occupy. Nowhere else in this country can sepulchral art through seven centuries be studied so fully: nowhere else is there such a representative concentration of sculpture.

The cosmopolitan tradition inaugurated from the start persisted. It was not to France only that Henry III turned for his ideas; from Italy were brought artists and craftsmen to build his tomb and the Shrine of the Confessor, as well as to lay superb marble floors. North of the Alps Westminster Abbey alone can show the art of the Cosmati exactly as it is found in Rome.

Henry VII employed Torrigiano for his own effigy and those of his wife and mother. The stall canopies in his chapel are of Flemish, not English workmanship. Throughout its history the Abbey has embodied the best that each age could contribute and it is in the wealth of its contents no less than in the building itself, now restored and cleaned, that inexhaustible interest may be found.

King Henry VII, (by courtesy of the National Portrait Gallery). Opposite: Henry VII Chapel.

The Precincts and College Garden

L. E. Tanner, C.V.O., M.A., F.S.A.
Librarian and Keeper of the Muniments

Those who pass along Great College Street may have noticed the ancient wall which bounds its northern side. This was part of the 14th century Precinct wall of the Monastery of Westminster. As well as the Abbey Church itself, it enclosed an area which included – in modern terms – Dean's Yard, the Sanctuary, part of Parliament Square, St. Margaret's Church, the west side of Abingdon Street, and so back to College Street excluding the Jewel Tower which was part of the Palace of Westminster.

Within the Precinct more of the buildings of the Monastery remain than is generally realised. The Deanery, formerly the Abbot's Lodgings, contains the 14th century Jerusalem Chamber and the Abbot's Dining Hall now the College Hall. Passing along the Cloisters one comes to the Little Cloister, formerly the Monastic Infirmary, with the remains of the 12th century St. Catherine Chapel. The Canons' houses on its south side look over the College Garden which can claim, perhaps, to be the oldest garden in London for it was formerly the Infirmary Garden. Its east and south sides are bounded by the Precinct Wall and the west side by the classical facade of the Dormitory of the Queen's Scholars of Westminster School.

The School, which traces an unbroken descent from a small school attached to the Monastery, was re-founded by Queen Elizabeth I in 1560 to become one of the great Public Schools. Its buildings are grouped round Little Dean's Yard and include the Great Hall, once the Monks' Dormitory, and the beautiful 17th century Ashburnham House known to many during the 1939–45 War as the home of the Churchill Club. In its garden are the remains of the Monastic Refectory.

Dean's Yard, formerly known as The Elms, was the site of the Monastic Farm and Granaries. The range of buildings along its east side incorporated the monastic Guest Houses, the Cellarer's quarters and the original monastic Schoolhouse. These buildings, now partly used as Canons' houses, retain much of their 14th century frontage.

Opposite : The North Front of Westminster Abbey. Circa. 1730.

This page : College Garden showing part of Westminster School.

The Musical Foundation

Douglas Guest, M.A., Mus.B., F.R.C.M., Hon. R.A.M., A.R.C.O.
Organist and Master of the Choristers

The musical foundation of Westminster Abbey holds an important place in the long history of English cathedral music. Throughout the centuries, the high reputation of the Abbey's music has spread over the entire world and, at various times, some of the greatest names in English musical history have been closely associated with it: Orlando Gibbons, John Blow, and above all, Henry Purcell.

The Choir of the Abbey today consists of 12 Lay Vicars (adult altos, tenors and basses) and 36 Choristers, of whom 10 are called Choristers, 12 are Singing Boys and 14 are Probationers. The Choir is a fully professional cathedral choir.

The musical repertory is being continually widened and ranges from music of the 15th century to the present day. Fundamental to the music of the Abbey is the singing of the daily Services of Morning and Evening Prayer. But the Choir is constantly called upon to sing at great services of national and international importance, many of which are televised and broadcast. Through the 20th century media of gramophone records, television and broadcasting, the Abbey offers its music to the whole world.

It may well prove difficult in future years to maintain the Abbey's Musical Foundation at a fully professional level owing to the costs involved which are always on the increase. But we propose, should it prove necessary, to take steps to ensure that it should continue its long and splendid tradition.

The Precentor is the head of the Choral Foundation, but the training of the Choir and the practical direction of the music is under the control of the Master of the Choristers who is also the Organist.

The present main organ in the Abbey was built in 1937 by Messrs. Harrison & Harrison, and was first used at the Coronation of King George VI and Queen Elizabeth in May 1937. It has four manuals, 110 drawstops and 26 tablets. The Echo organ is in the triforium. The console occupies a central position on the screen.

In 1965 the British Italian Society presented an 18th century chamber organ in memory of Vincent Novello. This beautiful instrument was made by Snetzler and restored by Mr. N. P. Mander: it has the original case and pipework, but a modern action; it is fully mobile.

The firm basis on which the Abbey's music exists is, of course, the daily choral services and the many big special services. But it is our hope that this great Church will be a focal point of the Church's musical endeavour and a place where great music may be offered. As the years go by, it may be possible to establish it as a place where great choral and orchestral works and chamber music will be regularly performed. A pattern was set in the Handel Commemoration concerts towards the end of the 18th century when the Abbey was packed to the doors to hear the works of Handel. This important aspect of the Abbey's music is being revived and extended during the Nongentenary Year, and once effectively revived, we hope that it will be kept alive. The present custodians of the music of Westminster Abbey are deeply conscious of their great heritage, the result of almost unbroken musical development and evolution over many centuries. The Nongentenary Year presents a unique opportunity to the Abbey musicians to add still further to this development and to hand on their heritage enriched and strengthened.

Orlando Gibbons.

Henry Purcell by Sir Godfrey Kneller, (by courtesy of the National Portrait Gallery).

The Choir School

E. W. Thompson, M.A.
Headmaster of the Choir School 1947–65

The early history of the education of the Westminster Choristers is lost in obscurity, but, as with other monastic foundations, it is probable that the boys joined with the novices here in the singing of the masses and daily offices, as far back as 1170.

In 1479 there was a master of the singing boys in addition to a master of the grammar boys, and there is a record of the names of the choristers for 1511–12. The foundations of Henry VIII and Elizabeth I provided for the education of the choristers with the forty scholars of Westminster School. In 1846 the choristers were taught in a room at the King's Arms in Bowling Street (now Tufton Street). At the turn of the century an old house was taken on the north side of Little Smith Street while a new school was being built on the south side.

The present Choir School, in Dean's Yard within sight of the Abbey and facing the ancient buildings, was opened in October 1915. The school was evacuated to Christ's Hospital at Horsham during the Second World War, and subsequently disbanded until the close of hostilities. In May 1947 the school re-opened with 17 boys selected at a trial held on January 10, and 13 boys who had been singing with the temporary choir organised by Dr. Perkins (the Sacrist) and Dr. Peasgood (the Sub-Organist) to maintain the weekend services during the war period, joined the School.

The boys are chosen at competitive trials, which are publicly advertised, and they come from all walks of life. Apart from music, the aim of the School is to give the boys an education suitable for their future needs. Boys are prepared for public schools and grammar schools and coached for scholarships both academic and musical.

The boys are doing in choir something difficult and artistically adult, and they do it very well. This makes them happy and gives them poise. It seems to be a very good education and an excellent introduction to life.

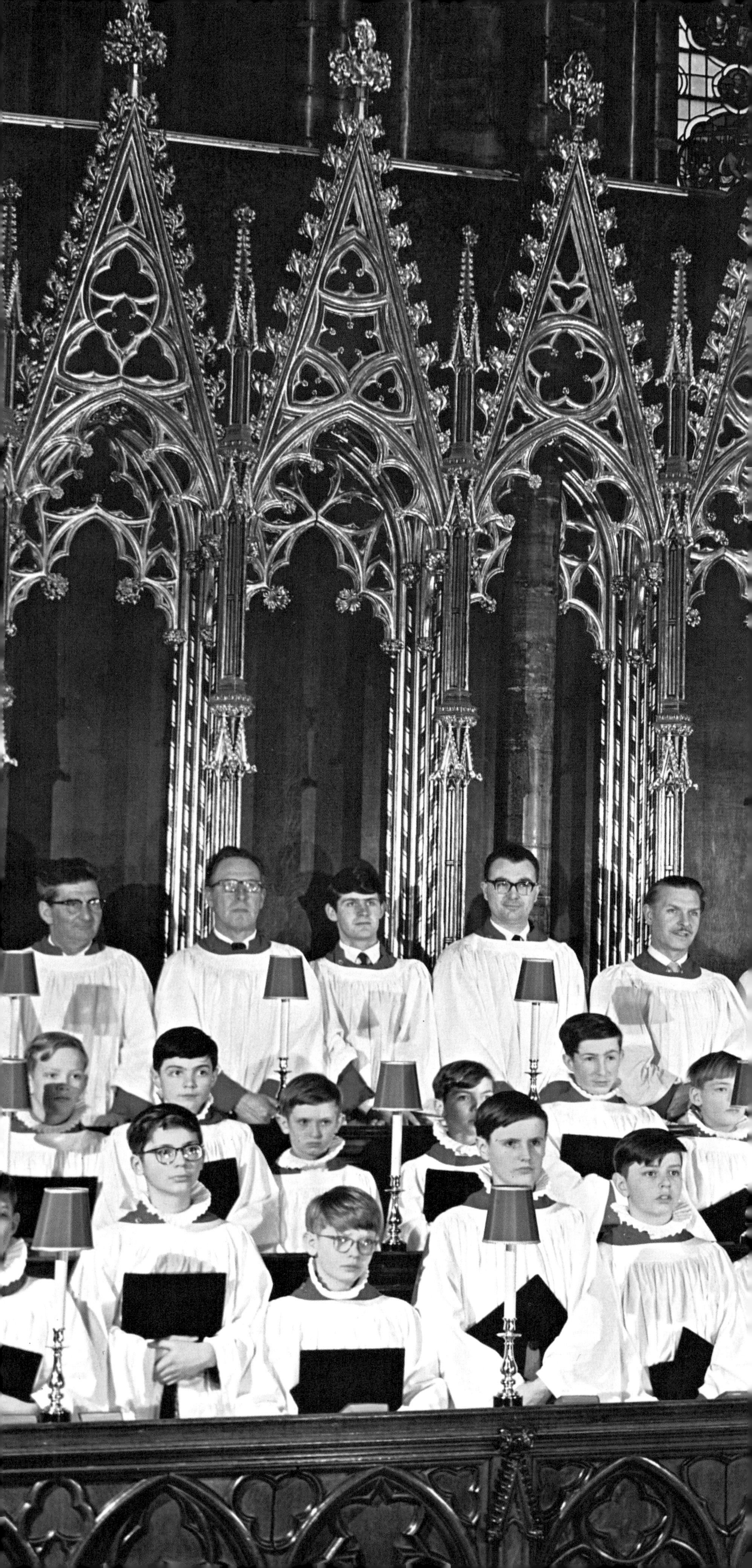

Westminster School

J. D. Carleton, M.A. Head Master

Edward Gibbon,
(by courtesy of the National Portrait Gallery).

Ben Jonson and Peter Ustinov, Warren Hastings and John Freeman, Thomas King (the original Sir Peter Teazle in The School for Scandal) and John Gielgud – these are some of the men who have been educated at Westminster during the four centuries since its refoundation by Queen Elizabeth I in 1560. Peers – and Anthony Wedgwood-Benn, the first peer to renounce his peerage – ultra Tories by the score and reformers like Jeremy Bentham and revolutionaries like Sir Henry Vane who was executed for high treason in 1662, George Herbert, Dryden, Cowper, Southey – these are some of the literary alumni; and on a lighter plane, G. A. Henty, A. A. Milne and Stephen Potter. The list of architects is headed by Sir Christopher Wren, of historians by Gibbon, of philosophers by John Locke. There have been seven prime ministers, ten archbishops and innumerable statesmen, soldiers, scholars and divines.

For its size, and it has never exceeded some 450 boys, Westminster has certainly produced its quota of famous men, for the little monastic school (which in origin it was) was within a stone's throw of the Court and the seat of government and in an age of patronage this counted for much. In a democratic age it is still stimulating to be educated near to the centre of national life.

Sir Christopher Wren,
(by courtesy of the National Portrait Gallery).

The School's buildings cluster around Little Dean's Yard. College, one of the earliest Palladian buildings in England is the house of the 40 Queen's Scholars, whose privilege it is to acclaim the Sovereign with shouts of 'Vivat' at a Coronation. Ashburnham House, with perhaps the finest 17th century staircase in London, contains the school library. A pedimented archway (1734), carved with names of former boys, leads to the Busby Library (1656) built by Westminster's most famous Head Master, Richard Busby, who is said to have kept his hat on when Charles II visited the school on the ground that he could not allow his pupils to think that there was any man greater than himself. The Great Hall, called succinctly *School*, had already seen 500 years of use when the school took it over in 1600 for it had been the monastic dormitory, built c.1090. The whole school was taught in it until 1884, and the walls blaze with the coats of arms of former pupils and the roof blazes with the arms of Head Masters. All are new, for the room was burnt in the great air-raid of May 10, 1941, leaving only the bare walls.

College Hall, the state dining hall of the Abbots of Westminster now serves a thousand meals a day to schoolboys. It is a 14th century building with a 16th century screen, and the tables are said to be made from the wood of the Spanish Armada – a tradition pious but improbable.

Peter Ustinov.

The Abbey and the Throne

The Rev. Alan C. Don, K.C.V.O., D.D.
Dean of Westminster 1946–59

The agelong connection between the Church and the Throne in England is nowhere more strikingly symbolised and exemplified than in the successive Coronation Services that have been held in Westminster Abbey ever since William of Normandy was crowned there on Christmas Day 1066. Indeed the continuity can be traced to a yet earlier date. For it has been said of the first English Coronation service, drawn up in 973, that 'it gave to the English Coronation Tradition, at its very beginning, a broad pattern, which it has preserved for almost a thousand years'.

It was not however until the 14th century that the medieval Coronation rite reached its definitive form as set forth in the precious *Liber Regalis*, or Royal Book, still treasured in the Library of Westminster Abbey. In those

The Coronation Procession of James II.

days the Abbey was a Benedictine monastery whose Abbot was independent of all episcopal authority, save that of the Pope himself. In the 16th century, the monastery establishment gave place to 'The Collegiate Church of St. Peter, Westminster', as constituted by Queen Elizabeth I in 1560. The Queen herself became the Visitor and the Collegiate Church, as a Royal Peculiar, remains to this day exempt from all episcopal jurisdiction. As Dean Stanley said 'so long as it remains the sanctuary, not of any private sect, but of the English people, so long the separation between the English State and the English Church will not have been accomplished'.

The Coronation of Queen Elizabeth II in 1953 served to demonstrate once again the close connection between the Abbey and the Throne. Through the medium of broadcasts and television, millions of people throughout the Commonwealth and beyond united in paying homage to their Sovereign, who in her turn dedicated herself, in her capacity as Head of the Commonwealth, to the service of God and her peoples, far and near, who acknowledge her as their annointed Queen.

Charles II embossed silver gilt flagon.

The Abbey Treasures

The Rev. Christopher Hildyard, M.A. Sacrist

Visitors to Westminster Abbey are often surprised to learn that there are no vestments, copes, or plate which date any earlier than the Restoration of Charles II.

The Abbey once possessed great treasures. In 1388, for instance, it was recorded that there were 307 copes alone (also 34 candlesticks, 9 crosses and 13 chalices and many other rich possessions). Much of this vast treasure was surrendered to Henry VIII in 1540 by force, and by 1553 all had been removed. The Abbey had been stripped bare.

In early Stuart days the Abbey once more became magnificently equipped, but during The Long Parliament, with Puritanism rampant, all was pillaged. Monuments and altars were smashed, the copes burnt and the plate sold. By 1644 the Abbey was once more empty.

These then are the tragic reasons why we are so poor in great historical treasures.

It was in 1661 that, once again, the Abbey began to acquire its present collection of treasures – although with the arrival of the Georges upon the throne, a terrible apathy descended upon the Abbey and our records show not one solitary gift for generation after generation. Indeed, it was only during the last few years of the 19th century that the Abbey once more began to come to life and advance to its present state.

There is little doubt that the finest of our plate is the silver-gilt Restoration plate of magnificent flagons, alms dishes, patens, chalices and other vessels. These are displayed in the Sanctuary every Sunday morning, except during Lent.

Perhaps the most romantic of our possessions are the magnificent pair of candlesticks, which stand on the High Altar, dated 1691 – romantic because they were given out of a bequest of one Sarah Hughes. She was the housekeeper to the under-master of Westminster School at that time. Little did this woman realise that her gift out of her life savings, would be seen, in so great a place of honour, by countless thousands for centuries.

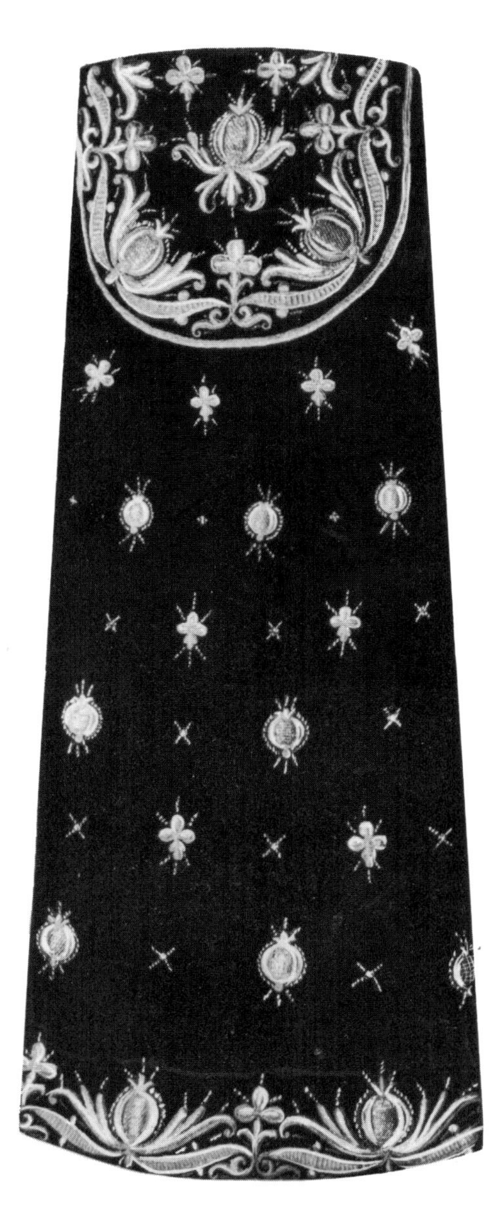

Charles II cope, in gold, silver and purple.

The copes made at the period of the Restoration are superb in 'cloth of gold' and in a deep red or purple velvet, powdered with pomegranates, trefoils and stars in silver and gold. Another lovely lightweight French cope dates from 1710, of blue damask silk woven with gold flowers. There are many other copes which have been provided from the traditional Coronation gifts of the Sovereign to the Abbey, some of great beauty. To these, we have now been able to add five superb white and gold copes, woven throughout in Lyons, woven on the very same looms used for Louis XVI's furnishing of Versailles. This has been made possible by a bequest of the late Mrs. B. N. Stuart.

Finally, one must mention the Cross of Westminster. It was given by an American, Mr. Rodman Wanamaker. It is made of gold, silver-gilt and ivory, and is studded with sapphires, and in honour of the 900th Year, Mr. John Wanamaker, his descendant, has added 72 diamonds. The result is magnificent. Thus the new world and the old world have met in the long, long history of Westminster Abbey.

Opposite: The Great Crosses of Westminster Abbey. The Abyssinian Cross; the Nave Altar Cross; the Cross of Westminster; one of the pair of candlesticks given by Sarah Hughes; the Ivory Cross.

A:R: GEORGII II. VIII. A:D: MDCCXXXV

The Most Honourable Order of the Bath

From the Saxon ages to the time of the Coronation of King Charles II it was customary in England to confer with ceremony a 'degree of Knighthood' and, from the Rite preparatory to it, it came to be denominated 'the Knighthood of the Bath'. King George I, in 1725, created a Military Order of Knighthood 'to be known as The Order of the Bath'. The Installation of Knights was provided for and the Ceremonies (having their allegorical significations) included that of a bath.

From 1725 a faithful record of the members of the Order was preserved in the stall-plates of the chapel of King Henry VII at Westminster Abbey (discontinued in 1812). The Order was enlarged by the Prince Regent in 1813 and three classes were formed – Knights Grand Cross, Knights Commanders and Companions. At the same time provision was made for the admission of a small number of distinguished civilians as Civil Knights Grand Cross.

In 1913, King George V commanded that the Ceremony of Installation, which had been omitted for many years, should be revived. The erection of banners and stall-plates was also revived at this time.

During the war of 1939–1945, to prevent damage by enemy action, certain parts of the woodwork of the stalls, together with the banners, were removed from the chapel, and it was not until 1947 that the chapel was restored and re-opened to the public.

Preceding page: The Procession of The Order of the Bath by Canaletto.

This page: The ceiling of the Henry VII Chapel.

The Benefactors

W. R. J. Pullen, LL.B., F.C.I.S.
Registrar

The glory of Westminster Abbey, its fabric newly cleaned and repaired, its furnishings, its copes, plate, crosses and candlesticks, indeed its very existence is due to its Benefactors over the centuries. These Benefactors – Royal; Ecclesiastical; well-known and unknown; rich and poor; men and women from all parts of the world, have given freely of their wealth or of their labours for the love of God and the enrichment of this Church wherein prayers have been offered daily for nine hundred years. The Abbey is truly theirs; it is also ours to preserve for our successors who in their own ways will surely add their contribution to the Abbey and its worship during the next hundred years, and we trust, for many centuries to come.

Among the registers and records of the Collegiate Church there is a fine illuminated book in which the names of the Benefactors are recorded for posterity. This book is permanently on view in the Norman Undercroft in the Cloisters. It includes the names of twenty-eight Royal Benefactors from Edward the Confessor's gift of one-tenth of his entire worldly substance in gold, silver, cattle and other possessions, to Queen Elizabeth II, our reigning Monarch and Royal Visitor.

Gifts are also recorded from various Abbots and Deans of Westminster and "other pious persons" including Sir Stephen Jenyng who gave a fodder of lead for the roof in 1501; William Caxton, a gift of the Liturgy inscribed on paper for use in St. Edward's Chapel; Richard Whittington, Lord Mayor of London, the sum of £6.13.0d.; Sir Julius Caesar, Master of the Rolls, £100 for books for the College; and in more recent times the following are noted:–

1908 George Montagu (9th Earl of Sandwich), a Christening Bowl of Silver.

1920 The Society of St. Faith – a chalice and paten for St. Faith's Chapel. The subscribers to the Appeal issued by Dean Ryle for the Fabric.

1934 Mowbray Vernon Charrington – a bequest of one-tenth of his residuary estate.

1939 Lord Lee of Fareham – two bronze candelabra adorned with numerous figures illustrating the history of the Old and New Testaments.

1948/57 Mr. J. A. Dickens £3,500 for various objects including the restoration of the feretory of St. Edward's Shrine.

1951 Gift of £45.7.8d. from a Mr. Price of Texas.

1953 The subscribers to the Appeal issued by Dean Don for the maintenance and restoration of the Fabric and the endowment of the Choir School.

1956 Two crystal chandeliers for the Jerusalem chamber by Mr. Guy Wellby.

1957 Miss E. E. Hodges – legacy of £25 for the Fabric Fund.

1958 Miss A. M. Mercer – legacy of £30,000.

1961/63 Timber from Queensland and Tasmania.

1965 Sixteen Waterford crystal chandeliers, and re-gilding of the Choir Stalls – gifts from members of the Guinness family.
$5,000 from Trinity Church, New York, towards the expenses of the 'Homage to Music', in 1966.
Embroidered kneelers for St. Faith's chapel by ladies of the precincts and other helpers.
Plants and shrubs for College Garden from various horticultural firms.
The installation of permanent floodlighting equipment by the Westminster City Council.

A new *Benefactors' Book* will record the above and other gifts to the Abbey, on the occasion of its 900th birthday and in subsequent years.

Not listed, but nevertheless not forgotten, are the numerous gifts, large and small, by the millions of people who come to the Abbey to worship, or merely to see it, and who by means of the almsgiving at Divine Service, freewill offerings in the collection boxes, or indeed by paying the charge for admission to the Royal Chapels, provide much of the annual income which is absolutely vital if the Dean and Chapter are to meet the ever increasing annual expenditure and balance their budget.

'. . . and some there be which have no Memorial who are perished as though they had never been and are become as though they had never been born. And their children after them. But these were merciful men whose righteousness hath not been forgotten. Their seed shall remain for ever and their glory shall not be blotted out. Their bodies are buried in peace but their name liveth for evermore.'

Ecclesiasticus 44

Overleaf: View of Westminster Abbey from the south bank. An engraving by S. and N. Buck, 1749.

5
6

7
8
9

Message from the Dean of Westminster

The Very Rev. Eric S. Abbott, M.A., D.D.

I hope that this Brochure will give to its readers a new insight into the richness of the heritage that is ours at Westminster Abbey, a heritage which, so far as we can, we desire to share with all who come to this great Church.

For come you do in your thousands and so much is the Abbey part and parcel of England's life that you feel it is yours, you claim it as your own.

This indeed is what we want it to be. It is a Royal Peculiar and it is ours. But it is also yours. As a result, we cannot be sectarian at Westminster Abbey; we must be in the true sense catholic. In a Christendom which is still divided we are Anglican, but we are for all, and only those are excluded who exclude themselves.

If you agree with me that in this sense the Abbey is yours, as you visit it in your thousands, what will you do when you come?

We talk of not being able to see the wood for the trees. Please do not say that you cannot see the Church for the tombs! Tombs indeed there are, so numerous that they have for some people confused or hidden the spiritual meaning of Westminster Abbey; here and there the monuments have spoilt its architectural style. But so gloriously has the Abbey been restored that your gaze is constantly lifted up. Look up! Do not try to forget the monuments and tombs, but let your upward gaze transcend them.

What will you do when you come? You cannot look up all the time. You are bound to study, cursorily or in detail, the tombs and memorials of the great and the not so great. Is the Abbey then a national museum? Is this the sense in which it is yours? I offer you a clue. The central tomb in Westminster Abbey is the Shrine of St. Edward, King and Confessor. The Abbey is packed, tightly packed, with history. But at its heart there is a Shrine, and it is *in its entirety* a Shrine; not a museum, though filled to overflowing with Memorials; but a Shrine, a sacred site, a holy place which abides though cultures change and empires pass away; a Shrine which bears in its fabric the wounds and buffeting of history, but has not been overcome. It must not be overcome. It must always be a Shrine. The Life of the Nation and the Life of the Church are here together, in partnership and in tension, and in some minds the secular and the religious aspects of this unique Church are more or less balanced. Therefore we must proclaim the Sovereignty of God over both Church and Nation, and the Lordship of Christ over all our life, both the so-called secular and the so-called religious. For this Sovereignty of God the Abbey stands.

We welcome you to this Shrine to join with us in our thankful celebration of its 900th year and pray for you that you may go out from it with the blessing of God. Will you in turn pray for us who are the present guardians of this famous Church, that we may bravely, faithfully and imaginatively discharge those tasks of Christian life and witness and worship which await us in the years to come?